Uncaged Wallflower

By Jennae Cecelia

Uncaged Wallflower

ISBN: 978-1535402668

Cover art by Islam Farid
You can find him at @islamsfarid on Instagram or IslamFarid.net

Uncaged Wallflower

For all of my dreamers-

The ones who are afraid to take out the key to unlock your stubborn cage.

This is your time to show the world who you are and what you can be.

I hope this book helps you to realize that someday.

Dear Reader,

Rather than speaking my mind right away, I was always more of a quiet thinker. I was an introvert. A wallflower.

To add to this, my mind was conjuring up negative thoughts I let flow out of my mouth with ease, ignoring the positive outlook I could have if only I could stop focusing on my flaws.

I wrote **Uncaged Wallflower** for those who feel trapped in the thoughts their minds produce, unable to express them with the rest of the world out of fear of critique or disagreement.

This is for those who need an extra dose of positivity in their day and a push to follow their dreams.

This is not a poetry book for you to read and relate to in a sorrow filled way. It is for you to read and say, *"yes, I can be better and I will."*

So please, don't ever feel like your opinion is less important than the opinion of others. Don't let your insecurities and anxious mind dictate your bliss. Never stop being a dreamer.

With love,
Jennae

Jennae Cecelia

Metamorphosis.
Feeling your wings
break through.
Growing into the best you.
Emerge from
your chrysalis.
Expand and learn
something new.
Don't get wrapped up in
your same old cocoon.

Live Your Life

How long are you
going to live
your life
for other people?
Answering calls for them.
Emails piling your inbox
with nothing but
bitching and moaning.
Making coffee runs
for six other people.
Curling your hair
instead of leaving it straight
because people told you
that you looked better
that way.
Pressing makeup brushes
to your face
because somehow it
became out of the norm to
show up to work
or events with
your bare face.
Because, how dare you
for showing your true colors.
How long are you going
to live your life
for other people?
Stop conforming to the norm.

I wonder how our souls are
picked for our bodies.
Is a good soul placed into a
bad body just to show others
not to judge by outer appearance?
Or, is a rotten soul put into a
beautiful body
to show others that looks are
only enough
until times get tough?
Either way, our souls are what
we take from this life to the next
and our body is what is laid to
rest.

No More Tomorrow

If it's not yesterday,
it's tomorrow,
or next week,
or next year.
I find myself living in thoughts
of the future more than
the realities of the present.
Hurrying through weekly tasks with
thoughts only embedded with
weekend bliss.
Contemplating if I said the right thing,
or if there was anything I missed.
I have to remind myself that I am
wasting present moments thinking
of a future that will either
come or not,
but that's out of my control.
So I take brief moments,
sit and enjoy the stars
and the way the grass
moves in the wind.
Because those are present moments
and I need to exist there more.

You may think
you are caged in
with little room
for growth,
but to every lock
there is a key.

And that's the thing
about people.
You can wrap them up
in kindness & love,
and they will still have
something cold to say
about you.

Surround yourself with people
who don't just ask
how you are doing.
Surround yourself with people
who make an effort to
make sure they are part of
the reason you are doing so well.

Your Words

If the words that spewed
out of your mouth
were the clothes wrapped
around your body,
the hair on your head,
the flesh of your skin,
would you think you are beautiful?

The Best

Life isn't about
always being the best.
It's about facing fears and
growing from them.
You don't have to be number one.
Just don't live a life full of,
"what if's."

Change

I have always hated change.
Even as a child I would
become frustrated
when the store would move
the aisle of dolls
to a different location
than before.
I hated when trees were
torn down and a large empty
space filled the home they
once owned.
I hated when the walls were painted
a new color and I would never
see the hue beneath it again.
I hated not being able to
adapt to change
as quickly as others.
But change is all around us.
We are always getting older,
looking older.
The building built five years ago
will need repairs.
And sometimes I wonder
if landfills are piled
with all the change people made.
Discarded items they lost attachment
to or needed to part with in order
to move on.
Change is always there.
Embrace the growth you are making.

Discard the rest.
Learn that change may
bother
you at first,
but it will save you in the end.

New Soil

Life will always have
horrible moments.
Moments you want to cry
into your pillow
and scream out the agony
that you've buried inside.
But there are always
more radiant days ahead.

Life may throw dirt on you,
but it's up to you to see
the good to come.
Grow in your new soil with
beams of happiness,
do not drown in tears.

Feelings

I used to fight tears
like they were lions
pouncing at me from a cage.
Biting my tongue so hard
it bled, because tears meant weakness
and that wasn't okay.
I remember the feeling
of a hard lump stuck in my throat,
From sucking in so much air
just to make sure
no water could escape.
My body was flooding itself with
unshed tears.
Like a dam that was
soon to break.
Tears showed weakness.
Weakness.
I'm weak.
I never knew tears
were normal.
Tears made me bleed.

We are broken people.
made up of,
cracks,
rips,
tears,
bruises,
cuts,
and scars.
But only a few choose
to pick up the pieces
and form something new
out of the shattered debris.

There is no such thing
as perfect.
No one is free from faults.
No one is ever going to
always say the right things.
The way we look is not perfect,
because perfect is a figment
humans make up in their
minds from pictures
of "ideal" men and women.

Dear You,

You made it.
You are here.
All the moments spent in agony,
wondering when the pain
would end and,
you are here.
You made it.
Your mind is beautiful
and brilliant.
You may not be everyone's
cup of tea,
some people need cream
or sugar just to take you.
Others enjoy you pure in taste.
But neither of that matters,
because you are at a place
you once dreamed of as your escape.
Who knew you would love smiling,
pure, genuine smiles that didn't
hint at the firing thoughts behind
your eyes.
You want others to know that
their minds can feel
this wonderful too.
We made it my friend.
Now it's time for your breakthrough.

Comfort Zone

One life.
Many stories
to make.
A comfort zone
should no longer
hold you in place.

Unpredictability

Fear is attached
to unpredictability.
Fear of an expectation
not being met.
Fear of a momentous
time ending.
But for me,
the best things happened
out of unpredictability.
My mind used to limit my options,
leaving little room for new
ideas or endings.
I would call the unknown and
I best friends now.
Because the unfamiliar is my
path to my next great task.
I wake up with excitement
in my stomach thinking
of all the possibilities ahead.
Here's to living without the fear
of not knowing what is around
the bend.

I used to be envious of
the people who took all the
good kind of risks.
The ones who packed their
bags and stuffed their car
full of everything they would need
to start over halfway across
the country.
But now I am smiling
because that person
is someone I could be.

Believe that your vision is the
pathway to your success.
No dream is a fantasy until
you let yourself settle with
thought that it is.
You need to pave a path.
One that many follow.
A trail people continue down
for years to come.
Hatchet in hand to make
clearance of overgrown weeds
and stumps in the way.
A pathway that is run over
with footsteps of curiosity.
People wondering how you
got to this point.
How you made your vision
a reality,
when it was once only parked
in the depths of your mind.
How you were able to stay
positive and happy
even when you didn't know
exactly when your next
paycheck would come.
Let them wonder how you got
to where you are.
Let them be the ones to try
and follow the path you have
paved.
Grab your hatchet,
and start clearing your path today.

We are all works in progress.
The first draft of a book.
The blueprints of a house.
The child learning to read.

We are all works in progress.
We choose to finish writing out
a story untold,
building a house out of
bricks and wood
that once started out as ideas
on paper,
and reading chapter books
with ease late into the night.

We are all works in progress.
Slowly but surely coming together.
We are the ones who never give up.

Moments

We have finite moments
in an infinite universe.
Some that we count as
our best memories,
and others we suppress.
We are made up of moments.
The pictures hidden
between pages of books.
The concert tickets piling up
in a bin,
crinkled from when we shoved
them in our pockets and then
washed the jeans.
Life is beautiful for giving us
these moments.
We may be made of
cells,
bones,
and muscle,
but moments are what make up
our souls.
Embrace your moments.
The good and the bad.
Moments come too quickly,
and one day you will do anything
to have them back.

You could hate me with
deep passion
and I'd still love you
with full embrace.
This world just has
too many people
quick to blow you off
for your silly mistakes.

Let Me Tell You, You're Beautiful

At a young age, I felt the need to
protect people.
My soon-to-be friend who was
pushed around by the fourth-grade bully.
Who told her she was dumb,
and ugly.
I was at a loss because I wanted to be
liked by the other kids in class,
but I couldn't help feel a vast amount of
pain for the girl in the jumpsuit and
red glasses.
She was the outcast and I wanted
to cry right along with her.
As I got older these situations didn't
really change.
Although the settings were no longer
playgrounds or lunchrooms filled with
adolescents,
it was now an office with grown adults
competing for a higher role.
It was the guys at the bar on a Saturday
night,
laughing at the girls with a little extra
weight
who were just trying to enjoy drinks
without stares of disgust.
It was the women being cheated on
because the temptation was too strong
for their unfaithful men.
I feel people's pain, and I want to rescue
them.
I want to tell them they are better than
the images people have of them.
That they are beautiful.

———

Shadows

The shadows looming in
the corners wore colors
similar to bruises.
No way of knowing
when the darkness would end.
Heart racing in your chest.
Staccato breaths.
Sweat staining your palms.
Darkness came in random spouts.
Dripping slowly,
or rushing fast.
Hot or cold,
it was never known.
Oh, how darkness could find you.
Darkness could find you knee deep
in happiness and come slap you
back into the reality of the hate.
Run fast, my friend.
Don't let the darkness catch you today.
Don't let the darkness overtake.

I was the candle that stayed lit
even in the
d
o
w
n
pour of rain.
The flame, never getting weak
from outside pressure.
I will never decrease my fire
that everyone tries to put out.
They are just afraid the light
inside of me might destroy them.

My Path To You

In life,
you are given
paths to choose.
Some are perfectly paved
with flowers
and directions
at each bend.
Others have
overgrown grass
with dirt
and no definite map.
Each brings forth
adventures,
excitement,
or dead ends.
Follow each path
with passion
because you don't know
where you could be lead.
Of all the paths
I have gone down
with bumps,
sharp turns,
dead ends,
and flowers,
my favorite was the one
that lead me to you.

Change Is Inevitable

I thought I would go
to a four-year college
a couple states away.
I thought I would have roommates
and attend parties
I would only pretend to like.
I thought I would eat bland cafeteria food
and shower around 10-15 other girls.
I thought I would study in my 12x12
room
under a desk lamp,
and walk to and from class all day.
I thought my weekends would be filled
with late nights with friends that would
one day be the bridesmaids
in my wedding.
These were things I wanted.
Instead, I went to college ten minutes
from my house.
My roommates were my parents,
and the only "parties" I had on the
weekends were drinking wine and
watching
some overly dramatic *Lifetime* movie
with my mom.
I ate food that was handed out drive-thru
windows or cooked on the stove
in my kitchen.
I studied occasionally but mostly just
relied on my good memory to help me
pass my classes.
The reality is,

—

I thought a lot of things
at the age of 18.
And the way things
turned out at that time,
I thought were disappointing.
But now, I am grateful
I didn't get all the things
I wanted.
I am glad I was different
from most of my peers.
Be open to different things.
Bumps in the road
may actually be
exactly the alteration
you need.
Change is inevitable,
but it is up to you
to grow with it
and make it as ideal
as you can.

No More Silence

If you feel like you have to be silent,
let me be the first to say you don't.
And if you want to be quiet,
let me be the first to say that is okay.
But, make sure your silence is your
choice
and not because you are scared
of what your voice may say.

Journey

Life is a journey,
full of wonder and worry,
but today I am at peace.
My mind will no longer
over-analyze the past or
stress about the unknown ahead.
I am present in the moments
in front of my eyes.

Villian

Who told you to be quiet?
Who told you
the best place to be
was off in the corner of the room
as far away from
human interaction
as possible?
Who made you feel like
your words didn't matter?
Who laughed at the thoughts that
you shared
after building up
the courage to speak?
I'm telling you to not be quiet.
Be loud and be known.
Talk to the people who seem
louder than you.
Share the thoughts dancing in
your brain with confidence
and ease.
Whoever told you
that you didn't matter
and neither did your opinion,
I'm encouraging you
to be the hero
taking over that villain.

My Mind

I used to think my mind
must be made up of
storm clouds,
lightning,
flooded rain,
and thunder.
But you helped me realize
what I truly embodied:
green grass,
sunshine,
blue skies,
crisp air.
Some days, there are still
sprinkles of rain
and a cloud or two.
But I am no longer near
that awful typhoon.

100%

You need to **realize** that
you deserve the best.
If the "love" **you** receive
is nothing but deception
and unpredictability,
only to be masked by your
wide eyes
and big heart,
please know you can leave.
Don't use comfort as a reason to stay.
No relationship **should** ever be a
90/10 type of love.
Find someone who gives it their all
and matches your efforts.
Look at the relationship
you **have** right now.
If they aren't giving their **100%**,
it's time for it to end.

Killing Fear

I used to be confined to the comfort,
of my house or bed.
The places I thought couldn't hurt me,
where I hid instead.
From people who took too many glances,
or the chance of having actual fun.
Fear used to consume my whole body,
but I killed fear with freedom
and now fear and I are done.
I now use my bed for sleeping,
and my home as a quick stop
after a busy day.
My head creates thoughts of happiness
instead of playing the same scene over
and over in pain.

Stars

Out of all the stars,
you were the one he looked toward
at night.
Never knowing that to him, you shone
brighter than the rest.
Even if there was an overabundance
of bigger or brighter stars,
you were always the one his eyes fell to.
The light he trusted would guide him.
The one he searched for even on
the most overcast of evenings.
I bet if you didn't spend time
comparing your qualities to the others,
you would have felt his eyes
always locked on you.
But remember, he is the one who
knew you shone,
even before you did yourself.

It's Okay To Ask Why

I was envious of the
honor roll students
as I stared at my C's.
I was the student
who needed to ask,
"what" or, "why"
instead of doing the
task with ease.
I later learned there is
nothing wrong with being
the student who raises
your hand with a question
instead of the answer.

Express Her Problems

She grew up thinking
strength meant not
being vulnerable.
Putting on her best poker face.
She fought the, "I love myself,
no, I hate myself" blues.
She never understood the people
who would cry at movies.
How could they dare show
such emotion in public?
Didn't they know sobs like that
were meant only for their
pillow?
She thought she was strong
because she didn't show her fears.
Didn't talk about her problems.
Because, if she didn't talk about
her issues, then they didn't exist,
right?
That girl wasn't strong.
She was broken
and torn, a bird slowly
having each feather plucked.
Soon she was going to crash and burn.
She didn't need to bottle up the
problems,
because problems weren't meant
to be kept in her head.
One small shake of that bottle
and the explosion of emotions
will be unstoppable.

———

Pop the Champagne

I wasn't meant to have a life
filled with 8 am wake-up calls
and 5 pm drives home
during rush hour.
I was meant to have a life filled with
unexpected mornings that lead to
unforgettable nights.
And even if right now I eat cheap
take out three nights a week,
one day I will be toasting
with overpriced champagne
to a life I knew
I was meant to lead.

Wandering Soul

You have a wandering soul
that is searching for a place
to call home.
Flying with the wings of
your heart.
Looking for a location
to land on.
For an attentive spirit to
capture your bad thoughts
and turn them into
healthy ones.
But his arms spread wide open
aren't a place to come in for
landing.
He wants to listen in order to
further his advantage
of getting into more than just
your mind.
Your wandering soul needs
to find a home within yourself.
Take time to rest and glide.

Letting People Go

It's hard to let go of people.
We anchor ourselves their flesh.
We grow to love their smile,
laugh, sense of humor,
and the familiarity
of their presence.
It's not until we start to do the
little things that we feel the pain
of their absence.
Like late afternoon card games
with an empty seat,
lunches at the place you both loved
but can no longer enjoy,
and one-sided conversations
with them even though they have
a lot to say back.
A glimpse at life without them is sad.
But you know they don't find home
here anymore,
so feel free to let their spirit fly.

Every day you get the chance
to work on being
the version of yourself
that you would be excited
to meet for coffee.

Forgiveness

I used to hold grudges
like a child clinging to their mother
on the first day of kindergarten.
I couldn't let them go.
The things people said to me
were stored in individual files
in my brain marked with their name.
The *things I hate* file bigger than
the *things I love.*
People piling up like scattered
notes on a desk.
The grudges I held becoming
a dark mess.
I started organizing my thoughts.
Filtering out the bad
and pouring in the good.
I learned that I just needed to
forgive and move on.
Even if the people who caused
my negative thoughts never know,
I no longer have a grudge against them,
because I had made forgiveness my
home.

Nailed

1 nail in each foot.
Pinning you in place.
No pivot,
no escape.
Take out your nails,
with the claws you enable.
The scars will heal.
Holes will be filled.
Goodbye to you,
the mannequin.

I found love in sheets wrinkled
around his body as I lay next to him.
The way that he called me
six different nicknames
but never once called me
a harsh name out of anger.
I found love in the way he drove
two hours with his hand in mine
every moment,
to surprise me with a gift he
researched for in secret.
In the way he never left me feeling
uncertain about what we were.
The way that I was his,
he was mine,
and we were us.
Together.
He called us a team.
I believe everyone needs a teammate.
One who supports you,
and isn't trying to compete
against you as an opposing rival.

Command Your Passion

Your clock begins to slowly tick
towards the end.
Your breaths become less frequent.
Your heart is beating at a decreased rate.
Think of the life that you have created.
How do you feel about that life?
Did you accomplish your dreams?
Did your bucket list have
items crossed off or was that just the,
"maybe one day, I don't know" list?
Were you fair to yourself and
your passions?
Are your grandchildren going to
tell stories about your life
long after you're gone?
YOU need to be doing what you love.
You NEED to be doing what you love.
You need to be doing what you LOVE.
Don't do it for the ones demanding
from you.
Do it for you.
Don't get stuck in the mindset that
you are no more than the people
who raise you or the place
you were born.
This world isn't made of eggshells.
Stomp on the ground and
command your passion.

Take Time To Yourself

Take time for yourself.
It is not lazy to stop the pen
from flowing for a day.
To put down your phone
and ignore answering
business emails.
To take a day to reply back
to messages or calls from friends.
Read a book,
shop online,
or take a long bath
with candles lit.
Taking time for you is healthy.
Your mind needs a break from
the hustle of your busy life.
Don't feel bad for taking moments
to yourself.
Spending a day away from
kids or peers.
Spend a day alone with only
your thoughts.

She Is Spring

She is now who she always
envisioned being.
The person in the reflection of
bodies of water and
mirrors on the walls are
no longer unrecognizable.
She looks just as she feels.
Her soul illuminates through
her skin.
The hate she once embodied
has overgrown to love.
Like a garden never weeded,
she is the flower budding
from the ground.
She is the grass that turned
from singed brown
to soft green.
She is the spring
right after winter.

Negativity is a chain reaction
virus that only ends
in devastation.
The problem is,
only a few are vaccinated

I Am Better Now

I know that if you saw me now,
you would recognize me.
You wouldn't turn your head
in surprise.
There would be no lift
of your eyebrow.
What you wouldn't
recognize though,
is that same girl
laughing and smiling.
I am no longer a victim.
I am no longer your puppet.
I am no longer the girl
you could reach out to
and know you would receive
a quick response.
I hated the person
you turned me into.
Today I am strong.
Today I am worthy.
Today I am successful.
I don't hate you, though.
Because, hate is a feeling and
I feel nothing for you.

Caged

I felt bad for the bird
in its cage that would
look out through its bars
at the blue sky
and trees.
I, too, felt like
I was looking out at
something I wanted but
couldn't reach.
Until you,
you were the one
to set me free.

You can pluck me
like a dandelion and
hope I never come back.
But I always do.

-I am a beautiful weed

The problem with being
sentimental
is that the breakup
is only the beginning
of the hurt.
Replacing his sweatshirt
that you wore
on chilly days,
that smelled like
hugs and bar soap,
was like ripping out
another chunk of your heart.
But I promise you,
the next sweatshirt will
feel better,
smell better,
love better,
than the one before.

-you will find the one

Resolutions

5, 4, 3, 2, 1......
The clock ticks down
to a time yet begun.
Pens tracing paper with ink
bleeding ambition
and new beginnings.
A kiss to seal a pressed envelope
filled with hope.
Resolutions have a stigma of failing.
Starting with full force and then
crashing in catastrophe.
Don't wait until December 31
to start being or doing what
it is you dream of.
Pretend there is no recollection
of time at all.
Just start,
and don't be sad
if at first it doesn't work.
Start over the next day.
That's the beauty of life,
we have every day to
gain and be better.

I write for the dreamers,
and the strong believers,
that we can conquer
our demons,
while wearing flowers
in our hair
and smiles on our faces.

~

Acknowledgements

Thank you to everyone who has ever
supported me along my journey.
To my readers who bought my first book,
Bright Minds Empty Souls, your
comments, and kind messages make me
so genuinely happy.
You showed me that the work I created
could be loved by many people for
multiple reasons and for that, thank you
again.
To my family, my love, and my best
friends, thank you for the never-ending
encouragement.
And to my grandma who is now in heaven,
the last time you responded to me as you
lay in your hospice bed, I told you I was
writing this book and you smiled so big.
Although you aren't here to read it, I
promise I'll read it to you someday.

Jennae Cecelia

~

To Read More Work by Jennae Cecelia, check out her other three poetry books:

Bright Minds Empty Souls

I am More Than a Daydream

Uncaged Wallflower Extended Edition

Jennae Cecelia

About The Author

@JennaeCecelia
JennaeCecelia.com

Jennae Cecelia is the self-published author of the poetry book, Bright Minds Empty Souls. Expressing herself through art – writing, drawing, painting, photography, has always been one of her strongest passions. It allows for her to share her emotions in non-traditional ways.
Jennae is well known for her poetic soul and vitality. With years of unpublished work, she is most excited about creating ways to further enhance her reader's experience. To continue to develop her writing style, the JC Collection is a compilation of poems based on using negative human emotion as a force of good.

CPSIA information can be obtained
at www.ICGtesting.com
Printed in the USA
LVHW02s2119041117
554943LV00001B/3/P